PRAY! WHAT DO I SAY?

A 21 Day Devotional for Kids

BY BETSY ADAMS

ILLUSTRATED BY CATHY HALL

FOUR:14 PUBLISHING

FORNEY, TEXAS

Pray! What Do I Say? A 21-Day Devotional for Kids

Text and Illustrations copyright © 2023 Betsy Adams
Published by Four Fourteen Publishing
All rights reserved.

No part of this publication may be reproduced, distributed, or transmitted in any form or by any means, including photocopying, recording, or other electronic or mechanical methods, without the prior written permission of the publisher, except in the case of brief quotations embodied in reviews and certain other noncommercial uses permitted by copyright law. The moral right of the author and illustrator has been asserted.

Cover design by

Illustrations by Cathy Hall

Hardback ISBN: 979-8-89109-532-8

Paperback ISBN: 979-8-89109-323-2

eBook ISBN: 979-8-89109-324-9

Library of Congress Control Number: 2023950129

Scripture quotations marked (NIV) are taken from the Holy Bible, New International Version®, NIV®. Copyright © 1973, 1978, 1984, 2011 by Biblica, Inc.™ Used by permission of Zondervan. All rights reserved worldwide. www.zondervan.com

Scripture quotations marked (KJV) are taken from the Holy Bible, King James Version (Public Domain).

Scripture quotations marked (MSG) or "The Message" are taken from The Message. Copyright 1993, 1994, 1995, 1996, 2000, 2001, 2002. Used by permission of NavPress Publishing Group. http://www.navpress.com

Scripture quotations marked "ICB" are taken from the International Children's Bible®. Copyright © 1986, 1988, 1999 by Thomas Nelson. Used by permission. All rights reserved.

Scripture and/or notes quoted by permission. Quotations designated (NET) are from the NET Bible® copyright ©1996-2016 by Biblical Studies Press, L.L.C. All rights reserved. https://netbible.com/copyright/

Scripture quotations marked (NLT) are taken from the Holy Bible, New Living Translation, copyright © 1996, 2004, 2007 by Tyndale House Foundation. Used by permission of Tyndale House Publishers, Inc., Carol Stream, Illinois 60188. All rights reserved. http://www.newlivingtranslation.com. http://www.tyndale.com

Scriptures taken from the New Century Version®. Copyright © 2005 by Thomas Nelson. Used by permission. All rights reserved.

Scripture quotations taken from the New American Standard Bible® (NASB) Copyright © 1960, 1962, 1963, 1968, 1971, 1972, 1973, 1975, 1977, 1995 by The Lockman Foundation. Used by permission. www.Lockman.org

DEDICATION

Author Dedication

To Mammy and Mom–our prayer warriors

Illustrator Dedication

To my family–who always surround me with love and support. To God be the glory.

NOTE TO PARENTS

Prayer is an ongoing process of turning our attention to God. It is a gift, an opportunity to talk to and listen to our Heavenly Father. Although it comes comfortably for some, it remains a mystery to many. There are days my prayers consist of wants and wishlists, and days I invite God to my own private pity party. I stumble over words. I talk too much, and I tend to be a little bossy. My mind wanders from the dust bunnies dancing in the warm rays of sunlight to the agenda nagging for my attention. But even with my imperfect prayers, I know God is listening and anticipating my participation in our conversation.

Even if you have a handle on prayer, teaching your children how to pray is often challenging. While some children find it natural to carry on a conversion with God, others wonder what to say. Bottom line, we want our kids to grow up talking to Jesus, and the two most important things you can do to help are:

- let them see you pray
- let them hear you pray

Prayers are purposeful, personal, and full of personality. We want our children to know their prayers are unique to them, a conversation between them and a loving Father. But we can also guide them on prayer so that it is both natural and powerful. Jesus modeled prayer for us, and we begin with this tool.

Matthew 6:9-13 KJV

Our Father which art in heaven, Hallowed be Thy name.
Thy kingdom come. Thy will be done in earth, as it is in Heaven.
Give us this day our daily bread. And forgive us our debts, as we forgive our debtors.
And lead us not into temptation, but deliver us from evil:
For Thine is the kingdom, and the power, and the glory, forever. Amen.

This is the formal King James version of The Lord's Prayer, but I have to say, I LOVE how *The Message* ends this prayer. After "keep us safe from ourselves and the devil," it ends with these words to God, our Father:

You're in charge!
You can do anything You want!
You're ablaze in beauty!
Yes. Yes. Yes.

So join me, and let's encourage our children to pray.

DAY 1

The Lord's Prayer

Pray. Anytime. Anywhere. Sounds easy enough, doesn't it? But sometimes, we get so wrapped up in what to say that we forget *why* we pray. Praying is one of the biggest things we can do. It is a way to communicate with God—to learn about Him and from Him. Most importantly, the Bible tells us to pray.

Prayer is talking to God. Think about it as simply having a conversation. You have conversations all the time. Praying is as easy as talking to your best friend or favorite person.

In the New Testament, Jesus tells us specifically how to pray. Getting pointers from Jesus is a pretty good plan and definitely a good starting place. So before you move on, read The Lord's Prayer.

Matthew 6:9-13 NIV

Our Father in Heaven, hallowed be Your name.
Your Kingdom come, Your will be done, on earth as it is in Heaven.
Give us today our daily bread.
And forgive us our debts, as we also have forgiven our debtors.
Lead us not into temptation, but deliver us from the evil one.

Wow! That's a lot of words. It's okay if those words are confusing. Over the following days, we will break it down and talk about each part. You might even try to memorize it along the way.

Something to talk about:
What do you already know about prayer?

Something to write about:
Why do you think praying is important?

_____

_____

_____

_____

_____

_____

_____

_____

_____

Something to do:
This week, when you wake up each morning, say, "Hi God," just like you say "Hi" to your friends at school. Make Him your very first thought each day.

DAY 2

Our Father

Jesus began His prayer with "Our Father." These first two words are important because they make us family. You know Jesus is God's Son, but He doesn't say, "My Father." He says, "Our Father." Jesus is claiming us as brothers and sisters. God is our Father, too, and not just any father. God is the perfect Father. Unlike our fathers on earth, God never messes up. Not ever (Deuteronomy 32:4)! He is watchful and wise (Proverbs 15:3). He is powerful, protective, stable, and strong (Isaiah 41:10). He is devoted and dependable (Psalm 33:4). He is everything we need in a father, and He won't ever stop loving us.

Prayer helps you stay close to God. It enables you to build a relationship with your Heavenly Father. So when you wake up in the morning and say, "Hi, God," you can add, "Thanks for loving me."

Psalm 121:8 NIV

The Lord will watch over your coming and going both now and forevermore.

Something to talk about:
God is watchful. What does that mean to you?

Something to write about:
Write a "Thank You" note to God for watching over you.

_____
_____
_____
_____
_____
_____
_____
_____
_____

Something to do:
Tomorrow morning, add to your wake-up prayer,
"Hi, God. Thanks for loving me. I like that You are watchful.
I like that You know what is going on in my life. It makes me feel safe."

DAY 3

In Heaven

*Heaven - God's home
*heavens - space, where galaxies and stars exist

We may not know exactly what Heaven looks like, but we do know God is there. It is His home. This makes Him unique and different from our earthly fathers. He is our *Heavenly Father*. We know Heaven is full of God's glory. He rules in Heaven. He is the boss, the King. Heaven is perfect, with no sin and no pain. There's nothing harmful in Heaven, only love. We know it's an amazing place beyond what we can imagine or even understand. It's a place to rest and play. It's a place to sing, worship, laugh, and learn. Heaven is a place of beauty and peace where we will praise and honor God.

Kind of exciting, isn't it? And even better, if you believe Jesus is the Son of God, died for your sins, and rose again, you get to spend eternity with God. That means you will spend forever in the most perfect place. Sounds heavenly, doesn't it?

Psalm 19:1 NIV

The heavens declare the glory of God;
the skies proclaim the work of His hands.

 **Something to talk about:**
What do you think Heaven will look like?

Something to write about:
Write some words about or draw a picture of the most beautiful place you've seen.

_____
_____
_____
_____
_____
_____
_____
_____
_____
_____

 Something to do:
This week, look for amazing things in the heavens and thank God for them (such as the stars, a rainbow, funny-shaped clouds, etc.).
"Hi, God. Thank You for the warm sun and…"

6

DAY 4

Hallowed Be Your Name

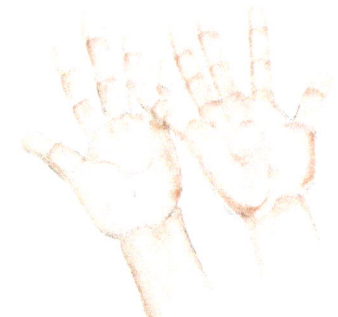

hallow - to honor as holy

"Hallowed be Your Name" means God's name should be honored or kept special. When we speak His name, we say it with great respect. Exodus 20:7 says, "You must not use the name of the Lord thoughtlessly" (ICB). This is one of the 10 Commandments, so we know it is very important. I like the word "thoughtlessly." This reminds us never to be careless with God's name. We do not use His name in a silly or disrespectful way.

When we use His name, we have His attention. He is listening. We honor Him by remembering who He is. The Bible tells us He is Almighty God, the Bread of Life, the Comforter, the Deliverer, the Great Physician, the Truth, the Rock, the Holy One, the Helper, the Everlasting King. He is many things to us, and His name is the most important name above all names.

To honor God is to love and serve Him. You can do this daily. When you read your Bible and pray, you honor God. When you praise and worship God, you honor Him. When you enjoy His creation, trust His plan for you, find joy in your day, and serve others, you honor God and His name.

1 Corinthians 10:31 NIV

So whether you eat or drink or whatever you do,
do it all for the glory of God.

Something to talk about:
Talk about the names and titles of God and which one means the most to you.

Something to write about:
Write about how you will honor God this week.

___

Something to do:
Remember to show God respect when you pray and honor Him with your words and actions. "Hi, God. You are my Rock, my Shield, my Father, my Comforter. Thank You for being all these things to me. Help me honor You with my words and actions."

DAY 5

Your Kingdom Come

Every kingdom has a ruler. A good king makes reasonable rules and protects his people. He brings order to his kingdom. God is *THE* King over all kings, and His Kingdom is perfect. When we pray, "Your Kingdom come," we are asking God to be the ruler of our lives—to be our King. We are choosing to support our King by honoring His ways. If we want to honor God's ways, we must know His ways. We get to know God better by going to church, reading the Bible, and praying.

Accepting God as your King means you choose to obey Him. His Kingdom rules are there to guide and protect you. The Bible contains instructions on how to live a godly life and make Him your King. Exodus 20 is a good place to start. That's where you'll find the 10 Commandments. You can be careful with your words, obey your parents, help others, share what you have, and spend time with God.

So, when you say, 'Your Kingdom come,' you ask God to be ruler of your life. You are saying, "You're in charge, God. I want to do what You want."

Matthew 6:33 ICB

The thing you should want most is God's Kingdom
and doing what God wants.

Something to talk about:
In movies and stories, kingdoms have good and bad guys. Talk about how you can be a good guy in God's Kingdom.

Something to write about:
Write down some things you can do to show others that God is the King of your life.

_____
_____
_____
_____
_____
_____
_____
_____
_____

Something to do:
Let's add to your prayer this week: "Hi, God. Thank You for loving me. Thank You for Your rules, the rules that keep Your Kingdom strong and keep me safe. Help me be obedient to You."

DAY 6

Your Will Be Done

*superior - higher quality, greater, excellent

When we say, "Thy will be done," we are saying, "Let's do it Your way, God." It puts us on God's team and shows we trust Him. We are agreeing that God's plan is the best. Isaiah 55:8-9 says, "Indeed, My plans are not like your plans and My deeds are not like your deeds, for just as the sky is higher than the earth, so My deeds are superior to your deeds and My plans superior to your plans." I like that God's plans are better than mine, not just better—superior! 1 Thessalonians 5:15-18 (NIV) says, "Make sure nobody pays back wrong for wrong, but always strive to do what is good for each other and for everyone else. Rejoice always, pray continually, give thanks in all circumstances; for this is God's will for you in Christ Jesus."

Whew! That's a lot. But you can do a lot. And you can ask God to help you. Doing it God's way means loving Him and loving people. Be kind. Be positive. Be thankful. So next time your brother or sister takes your favorite TV-watching chair, eats the last bowl of Lucky Charms, or brags about a good grade, remember to respond with kindness and help keep the peace.

Proverbs 3:5-6 NLT

Trust in the Lord with all your heart; do not depend on your own understanding.
Seek His will in all you do, and He will show you which path to take.

Something to talk about:
Talk about what it looks like to play on God's team.

Something to write about:
List some ways you can show love to your family.

_____
_____
_____
_____
_____
_____
_____
_____
_____
_____
_____

 Something to do:
"...but always strive to do what is good for each other and for everyone else..."
Think about this part of the verse and add it to your prayer,
"Dear God, help me be positive and helpful this week."

DAY 7

On Earth As It Is In Heaven

*Heaven - God's home

*heavens - space, where galaxies and stars exist

We know Heaven is perfect. Earth is not. Simply put, we hope for Earth to be more like Heaven. In Heaven, evil is exiled, friends are faithful, and kindness is contagious. The important thing for you and me is to help bring Heaven to Earth with our actions and words. We can't control what others do, but we can control what we say and do. In Heaven, the angels sing praises to God just as we can sing praises to God here on Earth. In Heaven, the angels serve God with complete joy. On Earth, we can serve God by happily serving others. In Heaven, the angels honor God with their obedience. We can honor God with our obedience here on Earth.

Every day, you have the opportunity to bring Heaven to Earth. You can be kind and gentle with your words. You can be helpful, happy, and honest. You can be a hard worker, a positive teammate, and a faithful friend. You can encourage others and cheer them on. Love God. Love people. Bringing Heaven to Earth begins with you and me.

Galatians 5:22 NET

But the fruit of the Spirit is love, joy, peace, patience, kindness, goodness, faithfulness, gentleness, self-control.

Something to talk about:
How can you help bring Heaven to Earth?

Something to write about:
Write two goals for this week—two things you want to do to help "bring Heaven to Earth."

_____
_____
_____
_____
_____
_____
_____
_____
_____
_____

Something to do:
When you pray this week, you can say, "God, help me be kind to others. Help me see good things every day. Help me tell others about You."

DAY 8

Give Us Today Our Daily Bread

When we ask God to give us our daily bread, it is much more than just food. It is about all our needs, physically and spiritually. Daily bread is everything from food and shelter to wisdom and faith. The good thing is, God knows our needs better than we do. We can trust Him to provide. Our job is to talk to Him about our needs. He wants to hear from us.

In Exodus 16, the Israelites were grumbling about not having enough food and didn't trust God to provide for their daily needs. This was after God delivered them from Egypt, opened the Red Sea for them to walk through, and provided water from a rock! Exodus 16:4 shows how God served up a fresh breakfast for them every morning, even when they doubted Him.

The Bible is full of stories about how God provided food, protection, wisdom, and strength when His people asked. If you look carefully and pay attention, you can see how God provides for your needs, too.

Psalm 23:1 ICB

The Lord is my Shepherd. I have everything I need.

Something to talk about:
Talk about your needs and how God has provided for your family.

Something to write about:
Make a list of things you need and want. Think about the difference.

_____

_____

_____

_____

_____

_____

_____

_____

_____

_____

Something to do:
Today, as you pray, add, "Thank You, God, for caring for my needs. I trust You to provide for me when I need courage, protection, shelter…"

DAY 9

And Forgive Us Our Debts, As We Also Have Forgiven Our Debtors

*debts - our sin

*debtors - those who have done something wrong to us

When we accepted Jesus as our Lord and Savior, we acknowledged that we were sinners. Bottom line, we all mess up. Sometimes we get angry at a sibling, complain about our chores, or disobey our parents. We are not perfect. Only Jesus is perfect. That is why only Jesus could die on the cross for our sins. And when He did, we were forgiven for our sins. All our sins. Yesterday's sin, today's sin, and tomorrow's sin. This should make us so happy that we are ready and willing to forgive others when they do something wrong to us.

So next time your brother breaks your favorite toy, your sister tattles on you, or your friend says something mean about you, YOU can forgive them. It's okay to say, "That hurt my feelings," but don't hold on to a grudge or anger. Remember, your family and your friends are not perfect either.

Ephesians 4:32 NIV

Be kind and compassionate to one another, forgiving each other,
just as in Christ, God forgave you.

Something to talk about:
God knows we mess up but loves us anyway. Nothing can change His love for us. Talk about what "sin" might look like in your life.

Something to write about:
List ways you can be kind and compassionate to your family and friends.

_____
_____
_____
_____
_____
_____
_____
_____
_____

Something to do:
When you pray, ask God to forgive you when you sin. Be specific. An example might be, "Dear God, I am sorry I yelled at my brother today. Please forgive me. Thank You for loving me."

DAY 10

Lead Us Not Into Temptation, But Deliver Us From The Evil One

temptation - the desire to do something wrong or unwise

First, let's be clear on this. God does not tempt us. Satan is behind every temptation. Once we are saved, we become Satan's enemy. He looks for ways to tempt us, push us toward sin, and make us mess up. This prayer is about us being watchful. We are asking God to help us see and avoid temptation. We are asking God to give us wisdom and protection. When we talk to God, we usually ask Him to lead us toward good things and to provide for our needs (our daily bread), but we also need to ask Him to lead us *away* from the wrong things. But when bad things happen, we ask God to give us strength and help us through the tough times.

God is always ready to help you, but what can you do to resist temptation? You can follow Jesus' example in Matthew 4: 1-11.

*Obey God (Matthew 4:1), *Pray (Matthew 4:2), *Memorize Scripture (Matthew 4:4)*

If Jesus did something, it's a good strategy for you. When you want to disobey your parents, skip your chores, or say something mean, it's a good time to pray and ask God to help you choose your actions wisely.

Psalm 119:11 NIV

I have hidden Your Word in my heart that I might not sin against You.

Something to talk about:
When do you feel tempted to do something wrong?

Something to write about:
What strategy will you use when you face temptation and why?

_____
_____
_____
_____
_____
_____
_____
_____
_____
_____

Something to do:
When you pray, ask God to help you avoid temptation.
"Father, when I am tempted to do something wrong, please remind me to honor and obey You and to choose my words and actions well."

DAY 11

For Yours Is The Kingdom And The Power And The Glory Forever. Amen.

I love this ending! This part of the prayer allows us to close on a positive note. It brings us back to eternity and to praise, back to where we started. In 1 Chronicles 29:10, we find a similar prayer recorded by King David. "O Lord God… may You be praised forever and ever. Yours, O Lord, is the greatness, the power, the glory, the victory, and the majesty" (NLT). If King David prayed it, we can too.

And then there is the powerful word at the end: AMEN. This means "so be it" or "let it happen." When we end our prayers with "Amen," we are agreeing with what was said. We believe in the importance of the words just spoken. We back it up. We stand by it. In The Lord's Prayer, we recognize God as our Father; we agree to obey Him, accept His will, and ask for forgiveness and protection. So. Be. It.

Psalm 69:30 ICB

I will praise God in a song. I will honor Him by giving thanks.

Something to talk about:
What is your favorite part of The Lord's Prayer?

Something to write about:
Write what you remember about The Lord's Prayer in your own words. Remember, prayer is just talking to God. Use the words you like and understand.

_____
_____
_____
_____
_____
_____
_____
_____

Something to do:
It's always good to start the morning with a shout-out to God.
You can pray, "God, You are the King. Thank You that I live in Your Kingdom. Thank You for providing for me, protecting me, and forgiving me. I choose to honor You by obeying Your commands."

DAY 12

Talk. Listen. Obey.

The Lord's Prayer is our guide. It reminds us to respect God as holy, to seek His will, and to ask for forgiveness, provision, and protection. I believe praying is one of the most important things you can do. Remember, prayer is you talking to God, and God talking to you. It's as easy as talking to your favorite person.

Talk. You don't have to use fancy words. You don't have to pray like anyone else. God loves YOU. He created YOU. Just be YOU.

Listen. You must be still to hear. In a conversation, you talk and you listen. In prayer, it means to sit quietly and think about God. Think about what you just told Him.

Obey. Remember that "Your will be done" part? When you talk to and listen to God, you will often feel a nudge to do something. Sometimes that something is easy, and sometimes it takes courage. The important thing is to obey.

Talk. Listen. Obey.

Psalm 46:10 NIV

Be still and know that I am God.

Something to talk about:
Talk about a time you did something nice for someone without being asked. Talk about why you decided to be kind. Do you think it was a nudge from God?

Something to write about:
Write about a time you heard God and obeyed.

_____
_____
_____
_____
_____
_____
_____
_____
_____
_____
_____

Something to do:
Take time to listen this week. Pray, "God, You are a kind and creative God. Show me ways to be kind to and creative for others this week."

DAY 13

Talk About His Goodness

The Lord's Prayer begins with, "Our Father in Heaven, hallowed be Your name." This is a great place to start. Remember, "hallow" is to keep holy, to honor. We honor God by praising Him. I begin my prayer time by recognizing the goodness and power of God. Psalm 86:8 says, "Lord, there is no god like You. There are no works like Yours" (ICB). Sometimes I just start by saying, "Father, You're the best!"

Think of all your favorite things—cuddling soft, sweet puppies, playing in the rain, chasing fireflies on a summer night, or winning your soccer game. The Bible tells us all good things come from God. Whether it is your talent, your friendly smile, or a double rainbow, all good things come from God. So begin your prayers with a grateful heart. Talk to God about His goodness, and then tell Him what you are thankful for.

Talk. Listen. Obey.

James 1:17 ICB

Every good action and every perfect gift is from God. These good gifts come down from the Creator of the sun, moon, and stars. God does not change like their shifting shadows.

Something to talk about:
Talk about some ways God is good to you and your family.

Something to write about:
List some of your favorite things.

_____

_____

_____

_____

_____

_____

_____

_____

Something to do:
Begin your prayer with a grateful heart. Talk to God about His goodness, and then tell Him what you are thankful for. "Dear God, You know everything. You can do anything. You are good. You are faithful. You love me. Thank You for…"

DAY 14

Ask For Provision

"Give us this day our daily bread" reminds us to ask God for provision—for all our needs. First and foremost, God provided a path to salvation, our greatest need. He sent His Son to die for us, but God didn't stop there. He provides for our physical needs and our spiritual needs. Prayer is a time to think about our needs and to ask God for specific things. Asking for His provision helps us focus on His love, faithfulness, and goodness.

What are your needs? You may be nervous about an upcoming test. You may be sore from an accident or a sports injury. You may be disappointed you didn't win a contest. Maybe you are lonely, miss your friends, or feel like you don't fit in. Talk to God about those things. Ask for healing, courage, or a good attitude. God's provision may not look the way you expected. He may not provide for you the same way He provides for someone else, but He does provide. He knows YOUR individual needs, and He knows the best way to support you. Ask Him for provision and trust Him to respond.

Talk. Listen. Obey.

Philippians 4:19 NIV

And my God will meet all your needs according to the riches and glory in Christ Jesus.

Something to talk about:
Talk about how God has provided for specific needs in your life.

Something to write about:
Write about a time you needed courage.

_____
_____
_____
_____
_____
_____
_____
_____
_____
_____
_____

Something to do:
You may not be asking for meals each day, a roof over your head, or warm clothes to wear, but don't forget to thank Him for those things. "Dear God, You have given me so much—food, family, friends. Thank You. God, You are amazing. God, today I need help with…."

DAY 15

Ask For Wisdom

Every day, I pray for wisdom. I ask God to help me make wise choices, to help me use my time wisely, and to help me use my words wisely. The Bible tells us God is ready to give wisdom to those who ask. So ask.

When we think about wisdom and people in the Bible, we usually think of King Solomon.

1 Kings 3 tells part of his story. God came to Solomon in a dream and told him he could have anything. Solomon asked for wisdom over gold and riches, and God was pleased. The people of Israel benefited from Solomon's wisdom and greatly respected him.

Asking God for wisdom helps you see things God's way rather than your way. And you already know God's way is better. If you have a decision to make or are unsure how to handle something, ask God for wisdom. Remember, you can pray anytime. Nothing is too big or too small for God. He wants to help with the little things and the big things.

Talk. Listen. Obey.

James 1:5 ICB

But if any of you needs wisdom, you should ask God for it.
God is generous. He enjoys giving to all people, so God will give you wisdom.

Something to talk about:
Talk about how it can honor God when we pray for wisdom and obey.

Something to write about:
Write about a time you didn't know what to do and tell what happened.

_____
_____
_____
_____
_____
_____
_____
_____
_____
_____

Something to do:
When you pray, ask God for wisdom and be specific.
"Dear God, I didn't know how to respond when the kid in my class made fun of me. Give me wise words to use next time."

DAY 16

Ask For Protection

temptation - the desire to do something wrong or unwise

"Deliver us from evil" is clearly stated in The Lord's Prayer. Temptation will come our way. Often doing the wrong thing is easier than doing the right thing. This is why we talk to God about it. Temptation is the desire to say things we shouldn't say, to go places we shouldn't go, or to do things we shouldn't do.

You might be tempted to argue with your parents, complain about a task given to you, or whine about not getting your way. You might be tempted to gossip or say something mean. Temptation isn't sin, but it can lead you there—you need to run from it. When you want to do something mean or wrong, talk to God. Ask Him for protection from temptation. Psalm 46:1 says God always helps in times of trouble. I Corinthians 10:13 says God always gives us an out when we face temptation. Ask God to show you the way out!

Talk. Listen. Obey.

Matthew 26:41 NIV

Watch and pray so you will not fall into temptation.

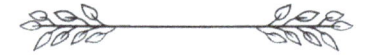

Something to talk about:
Talk about the things you know are wrong and how you can avoid those things.

Something to write about:
List some things you are tempted to do.

_____
_____
_____
_____
_____
_____
_____
_____
_____
_____

Something to do:
When you are tempted, frustrated, or angry and want to fuss or complain, pray right then. "Dear God, I know this is wrong. Show me the way out. Help me honor and obey You. Thank You, God, that you promise to help me."

DAY 17

Ask For Forgiveness

sin - an act against God's law or commands
blameless - innocent of wrongdoing
repentance - feeling sad about something we did

God sent His Son to die for us. When we accept Jesus as our Lord and Savior, we are forgiven. God sees us as blameless, but we still need to talk to Him about our sins. When we mess up, repenting and asking for forgiveness are important. Repentance is more than just saying we are sorry. It is a desire to change our ways—to do better.

Sin is selfish. It is choosing to do something against God's commands. You might say something mean, complain about your chores, fight with your brother or sister, take something that isn't yours, or tell a lie. You need to ask God to forgive you, and you may need to apologize to someone.

God doesn't want you to be stuck in guilt or shame. Prayer is talking to God about what you do wrong and how to do better next time. Psalm 103:12 says, "He has taken our sins away from us as far as the east is from the west" (ICB). Talk to God when you mess up. Ask for forgiveness, and repent. And don't forget to forgive others when they hurt you!

Talk. Listen. Obey.

1 John 1:9 ICB

But if we confess our sins, he will forgive our sins. We can trust God.
He does what is right. He will make us clean from all the wrongs we have done.

Something to talk about:
Talk about repentance and how just asking for forgiveness isn't enough.

Something to write about:
Write about a time you messed up and how you can do better.

_____
_____
_____
_____
_____
_____
_____
_____
_____
_____

Something to do:
Next time you mess up, pray, "God, forgive me for disobeying Your teachings. Show me how to apologize and do better next time. Thank You for forgiving me."

DAY 18

Ask For Others

The Lord's Prayer says, "Give us today our daily bread," "Forgive us our debts," and "Deliver us from evil." Did you see the "us?" Jesus is teaching you and me the importance of community, family, and friends. He is teaching us to care for others. Prayer is powerful. We are talking to a powerful God. The only God. The God who created everything and can do anything. When we see others in trouble or struggling, we should pray for them. Praying for others means putting aside what we want and focusing on the needs of those around us.

You may notice someone in your family is grouchy. It simply means they're having a bad day or upset about something. What a great time to pray for that person! You can ask God to help them feel better, to help them sort out their problem, or to find something to laugh about. I use that one all the time. When I see someone sad, I ask God to send them a big ol' belly laugh about something funny they see or hear.

You may know of someone who is sick, injured, or lonely. Pay attention at home, at the store, or at school. When you see someone in an uncomfortable or sad situation, pray for them. Prayer is a great way to love people. Then don't forget to listen. God may want you to be part of cheering up or helping those people.

Talk. Listen. Obey.

1 Timothy 2:1 ICB

First, I tell you to pray for all people.
Ask God for the things people need, and be thankful to Him.

Something to talk about:
God has surrounded you with people.
Talk about who is in your community and how you can pray for them.

Something to write about:
Write about a time you saw someone sad and what you did to help.

_____

_____

_____

_____

_____

_____

_____

_____

_____

_____

Something to do:
Be aware of the people around you who might need your prayers.
"Dear God, my friend is sick and can't come to school.
Please comfort my friend and show me how I can help."

DAY 19

Listen

Prayer is communication with God. Communication is talking and listening. Can you imagine if we did all the talking and never let our friends say anything? Isaiah 30:21 says, "Your own ears will hear Him. Right behind you, a voice will say, 'this is the way you should go,' whether to the right or the left" (NLT). God is ready to talk to us. He is ready to give us directions. We listen because He helps us make better decisions and gives us courage. We listen because we learn more about Him. God loves us, and we can trust His voice. The more time we spend with God, the easier it is to hear Him.

Just like you can pray anytime, God can speak to you anytime. You can have a conversation with God while you're brushing your teeth, riding your bike, or going to soccer practice. He will speak to you personally and in a way you understand. Psalm 5:3 says, "In the morning, Lord, you hear my voice; in the morning I lay my requests before you and wait expectantly" (NIV). I love that! It says we wait expectantly. This means we wait with confident excitement, so pay attention. God is going to tell you something. He may say, "I am with you today and always." He may say, "Be kind." He may say, "Don't be afraid. I've got this." He'll speak when He thinks you're ready, so be ready!

Talk. Listen. Obey.

Jeremiah 33:3 NET

Call on me in prayer and I will answer you. I will show you great and mysterious things which you still do not know about.

Something to talk about:
Talk about how you will be ready to listen to God tell you something.

Something to write about:
Write about a decision or need you have and how you will wait expectantly for an answer.

_____
_____
_____
_____
_____
_____
_____
_____
_____
_____

Something to do:
This week, start each morning with a prayer time. Mornings are busy, especially on a school day, but prayer sets the tone for the day. Praise Him, thank Him, tell Him your needs, then say, "Hey, God, what do You have for me today?"

DAY 20

Obey

Obedience. When we hear God's voice, we need to respond. If He tells us to be brave, we can face the day confidently. If He tells us to be kind, we keep our comments encouraging. When we hear God's voice, that gentle nudge telling us to do something, we have to be willing to obey. In The Lord's Prayer, when we say, "Thy will be done," we are saying, "Let's do it Your way, God."

God often asks you to do something hard, like apologize to your sister, stand up for someone who is bullied, or speak up when you see something wrong. When God speaks to you and gives you a command, immediately start thinking about how to obey His instruction. If you are unsure what to do, you can talk to your parents, grandparents, or guardian. God uses them to lead and guide you. He uses the Bible to instruct you. He uses prayer to speak to you. Pay attention to the things He has put in place to help you.

Luke 11:28 (NIV) says, "…blessed rather are those who hear the word of God and obey it." In Matthew 22, Jesus tells the disciples the greatest commandment is to love God with all your heart, soul, and mind. Then to love your neighbor. Love God. Love people. That is what God commands us to do. We do it best when we have daily conversations with Him.

Talk. Listen. Obey.

Deuteronomy 8:6 ICB

Obey the commands of the Lord your God.
Live as He has commanded you and respect Him.

Something to talk about:
Talk about how you can stand up for what's right at school.

Something to write about:
Write about a time you needed to apologize to someone.

___

Something to do:
Watch for ways to obey God this week. You can always start by obeying your parents! "Dear God, help me hear You this week. I pray my actions and words honor You as I obey Your commandments."

DAY 21

Talk. Listen. Obey.

Prayer is how we develop a relationship with God. We talk and we listen. The Lord's Prayer is a guide. It reminds us of things we can talk about to God, but you can't mess it up. Any time you talk to God or sit and listen for God to speak, you will learn and grow in your walk with Him.

A designated quiet time for Bible study and prayer is important. But don't forget you can talk to God anytime. Walking home from school, just before a game, while you do your chores, when you spend the night away from home—you can talk to God anytime.

You might have just played the best game of your life; you can thank Him for the talent and opportunity He has given you. You might have just played the worst game of your life; you can thank Him that there will be more games and ask Him to help you improve as you practice.

You might see something beautiful or have a great laugh with a friend. You can thank Him for those moments. You can ask Him to keep you safe, help you sleep, take away fear, give you ideas, improve your skills, help you be kind, make you wise, take care of your grandparents, help your little sister, give you a chance to share about Jesus, or allow you to help someone. As you can see, you can pray about anything.

Each day we have a chance to love God and love people. Each day we have an opportunity to be kind and learn new things. God walks with us every step of the way, so let's talk to Him throughout the day. He is waiting for you. He is looking forward to hanging out with you. He wants to hear from you.

Talk to God. Pray.

Psalm 66:19 NLT

But God did listen! He paid attention to my prayer.

Something to talk about:
What have you learned about prayer?

Something to write about:
Why do you think praying is important?

_____
_____
_____
_____
_____
_____
_____
_____
_____
_____
_____
_____
_____
_____

Something to do:
Pray. Anytime. Anywhere.

AUTHOR'S NOTE

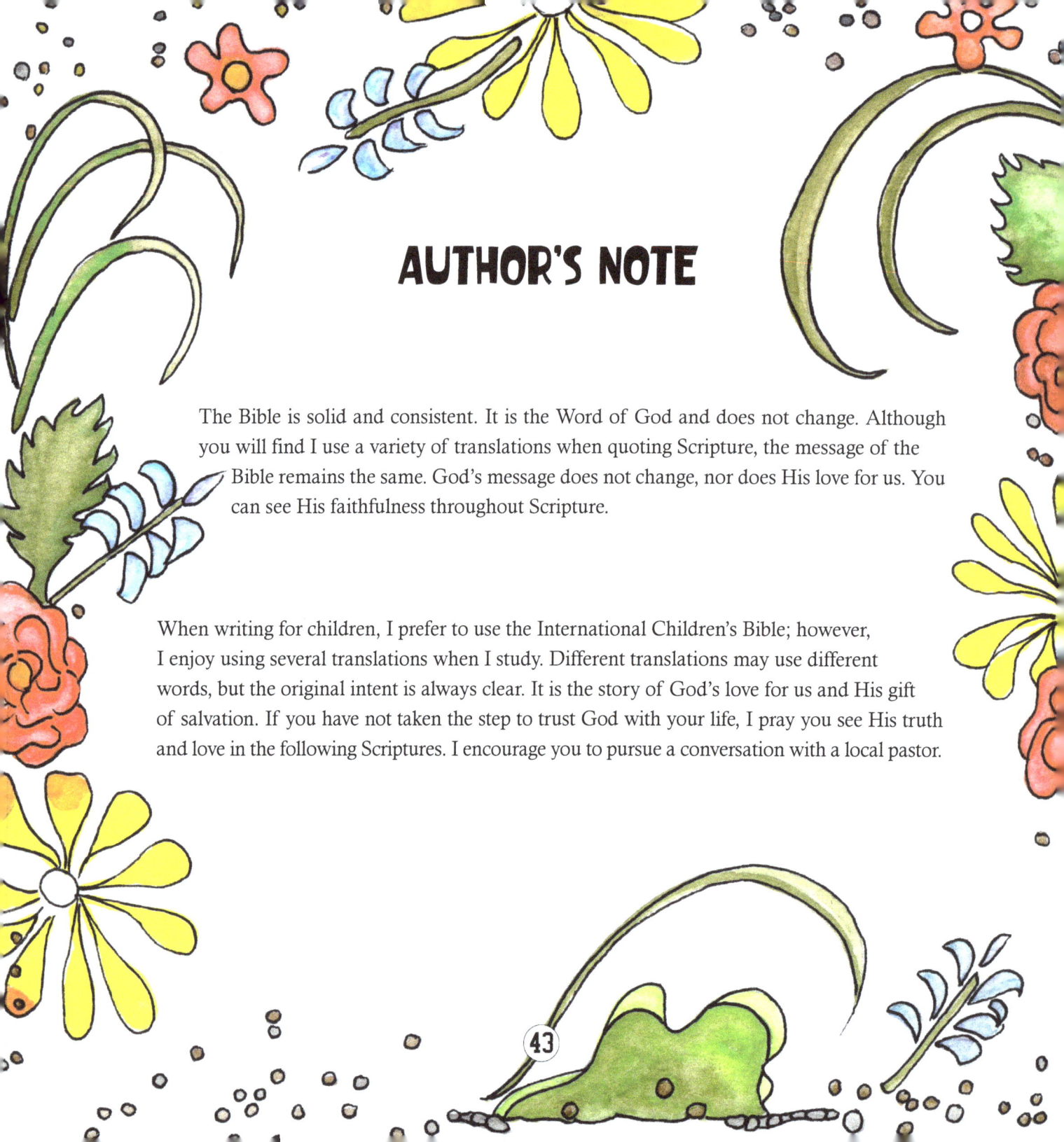

The Bible is solid and consistent. It is the Word of God and does not change. Although you will find I use a variety of translations when quoting Scripture, the message of the Bible remains the same. God's message does not change, nor does His love for us. You can see His faithfulness throughout Scripture.

When writing for children, I prefer to use the International Children's Bible; however, I enjoy using several translations when I study. Different translations may use different words, but the original intent is always clear. It is the story of God's love for us and His gift of salvation. If you have not taken the step to trust God with your life, I pray you see His truth and love in the following Scriptures. I encourage you to pursue a conversation with a local pastor.

Romans 3:10

"As it is written: there is no one righteous,
not even one…"

Romans 3:23

"…for all have sinned and fall short of the glory of God."

Romans 5:8

"But God demonstrates His own love for us in this:
While we were still sinners, Christ died for us."

Romans 6:23

"For the wages of sin is death, but the gift of God is
eternal life in Christ Jesus our Lord."

Romans 10:9

"If you declare with your mouth, 'Jesus is Lord,' and believe in your heart that
God raised Him from the dead, you will be saved."

Romans 10:13

"…for everyone who calls on the name of the Lord will be saved."

AUTHOR'S REQUEST

Thank You For Reading My Book!

I really appreciate all of your feedback and
I love hearing what you have to say.

Leaving a written review about this book, helps get "Pray! What Do I Say?" into the hands of more kids around the world.

Please take two minutes now to leave a helpful review on Amazon letting me know what you thought of the book:

betsyadamsauthor.com/review

Thanks so much!

Betsy Adams

AUTHOR'S THANKS

Thank you, Dr. Joe Paris, for your support with research and consultation.

You can connect with Betsy on Instagram @betsyadamsauthor or visit her website at betsyadamsauthor.com

Be sure and check out Betsy's devotional book, *Saved! Now What?* With young, new Christians in mind, the book is designed to share the next steps after salvation. Kid-friendly devotionals open the door for discussion on prayer, friendship, attitude, and Bible study. A unique journaling piece gives families a personalized keepsake of their child's growing faith. This 20-day devotional begins a basic discipleship process for children.

Read more about Saved! Now What? at betsyadamsauthor.com

Milton Keynes UK
Ingram Content Group UK Ltd.
UKHW051912091223
434034UK00003B/36